BOOK WORMS

GUESS WHO

Soars

Apple Jordan

mc Marshall Cavendish
Benchmark
New York

I have soft feathers.

They are brown and white.

I have a strong yellow beak.

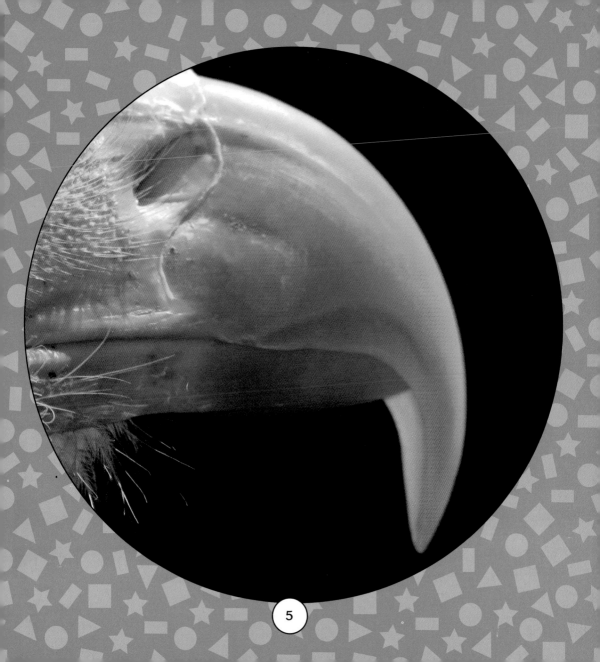

My eyes are amazing.

I can spot a fish from far away.

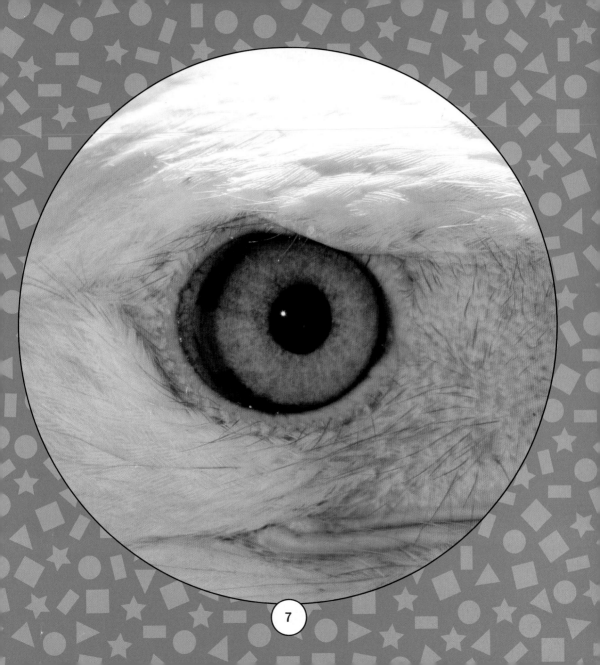

My claws are long
and sharp.

I use them to catch
my **prey**.

I lay my eggs in a nest.

I sit on my eggs to keep them warm.

When the eggs **hatch**, my babies are born.

They are covered in fluffy **down**.

I like to **perch** way up high.

15

I spread my large wings.

Then I soar through
the air.

Who am I?

I am a bald eagle!

Who Am I?

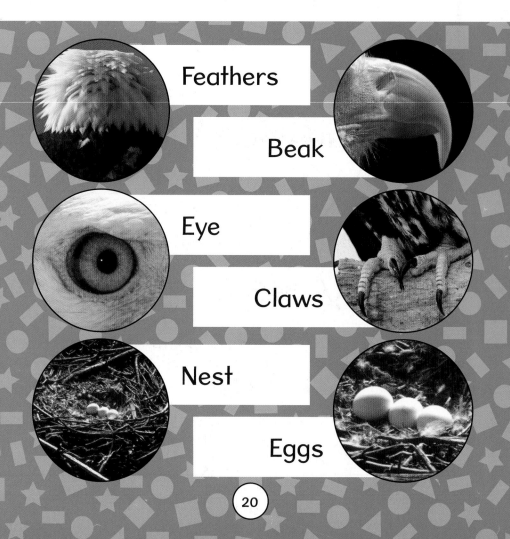

Feathers

Beak

Eye

Claws

Nest

Eggs

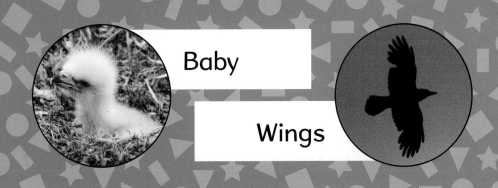

Baby

Wings

Challenge Words

Down (doun) soft feathers

Hatch (hach) to come out of an egg

Perch (purch) to sit or rest

Prey (pray) an animal that is hunted
for food

Index

Page numbers for photographs are in **boldface**.

About the Author

Apple Jordan has written many books for children, including a number of titles in the Bookworms series. She lives in upstate New York with her husband and two children.

With thanks to the Reading Consultants:

Nanci Vargas, Ed.D., is an Assistant Professor of Elementary Education at the University of Indianapolis.

Beth Walker Gambro is an Adjunct Professor at the University of St. Francis in Joliet, Illinois.

Published by Marshall Cavendish Benchmark
An imprint of Marshall Cavendish Corporation

Other Marshall Cavendish Offices:
Marshall Cavendish International (Asia) Private Limited, 1 New Industrial Road, Singapore 536196 • Marshall Cavendish International (Thailand) Co Ltd. 253 Asoke, 12th Flr, Sukhumvit 21 Road, Klongtoey Nua, Wattana, Bangkok 10110, Thailand • Marshall Cavendish (Malaysia) Sdn Bhd, Times Subang, Lot 46, Subang Hi-Tech Industrial Park, Batu Tiga, 40000 Shah Alam, Selangor Darul Ehsan, Malaysia

Marshall Cavendish is a trademark of Times Publishing Limited

Library of Congress
Cataloging-in-Publication Data

Jordan, Apple.
Guess who soars / Apple Jordan.
p. cm. — (Bookworms: guess who)
Includes index.
Summary: "Following a guessing game format, this book provides young readers with clues about a bird's physical characteristics, behaviors, and habitats, challenging readers to identify it"
—Provided by publisher.
ISBN 978-1-60870-429-3
1. Birds—Juvenile literature. I. Title.
QL676.2.J67 2012
598—dc22   2011000333

Editor: Joy Bean
Publisher: Michelle Bisson
Art Director: Anahid Hamparian
Series Designer: Virginia Pope

Photo research by Tracey Engel

Cover: Riccardo Savi/Getty Images
Title page: Accent Alaska.com/Alamy

The photographs in this book are used by permission and through the courtesy of: *Getty Images*: Yva Momatiuk/John Eastcot, 3, 20 (top, left); *Shutterstock*: Lori Skelton, 5, 7, 20 (top, right), 20 (middle, left); snake, 17, 21 (right); SuperStock: Robert Harding Picture Library, 9, 20 (middle, right); Gallo Images, 15; M. Cohen/Purestock, 19; *AnimalsAnimals*: Roger Aitkenhead, 11, 20 (bottom, left), 20 (bottom, right); *Alamy*: Accent Alaska.com, 13, 21 (left).

Printed in Malaysia (T)
1 3 5 6 4 2